Sally

Lehrwerk für den
Englischunterricht ab Klasse 3

Pupil's Book 3

Erarbeitet von
Martina Bredenbröcker
Jasmin Brune
Daniela Elsner
Barbara Gleich
Stefanie Gleixner-Weyrauch
Simone Gutwerk
Marion Lugauer
Sabine Schwarz
Anke Spangenberg

Unter Beratung von
Jane Brockmann-Fairchild

Illustriert von
Barbara Jung, Wilfried Poll,
Anja Boretzki, Gisela Vogel

Oldenbourg Schulbuchverlag, München

Inhalt

Hello 3

Colours and numbers ... 6

At school 8

Body and feelings 10

Toys 15

Clothes 18

Weather and days 20

Around the year 23

Family and friends 24

Drinks 27

Breakfast 28

Fruit 30

Pets 32

London 34

Farm animals 36

Summer 39

Robin Hood 40

Special days:

Happy Halloween 42

Merry Christmas 44

Valentine's Day 47

Happy Easter 48

Words 49

The happy kangaroo song

1 🔘 **Listen and sing.**

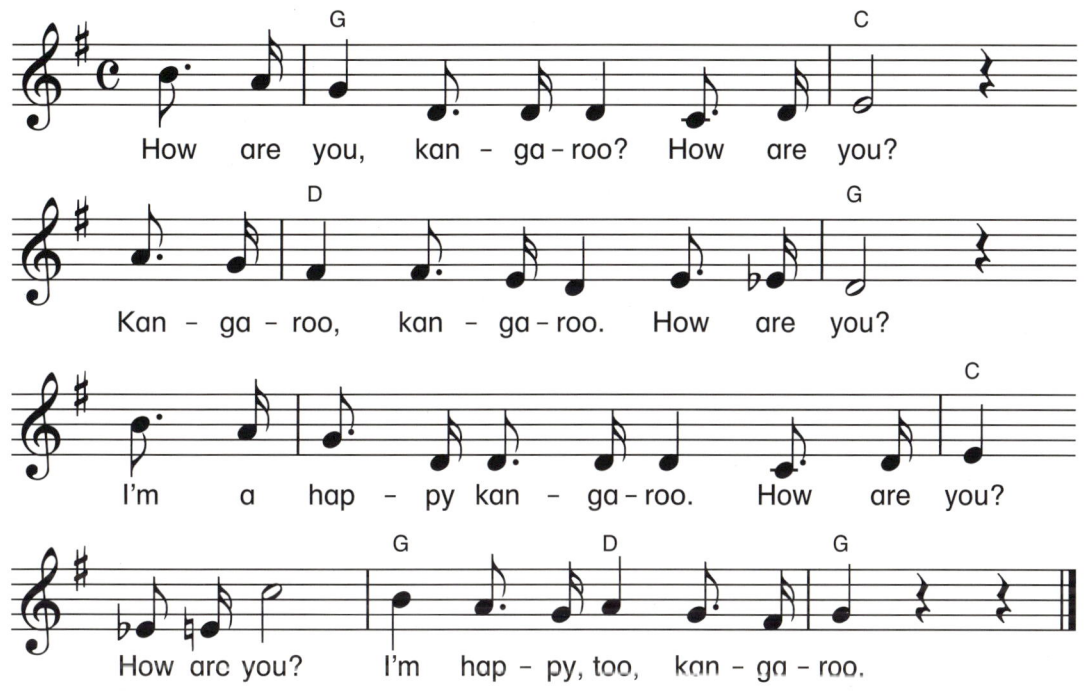

How are you, kan-ga-roo? How are you?

Kan-ga-roo, kan-ga-roo. How are you?

I'm a hap-py kan-ga-roo. How are you?

How are you? I'm hap-py, too, kan-ga-roo.

2 👦👧 **Ask your partner:** What's your name? How are you?

English all around

There are many English words in the picture.
Look and say: I can see …

2 Make a poster with English words.
Cut out pictures or words from magazines.

Group the words (sports, food, drinks, ...).

Mr Blue and Mrs Yellow

1 💿 **Listen and point.**

2 💬 **What colour is it?**

grey

pink

orange

purple

brown

green

3 👦👧 **Act out the story with a partner.**

CD 1.4

Sally's rhyme

1 📀💬 **Listen, say the rhyme and do the actions.**

One, two, three –
Sally, point to me!

Four, five, six –
Sally, let us mix!

Seven, eight, nine –
now let's stand in line!

Now comes ten,
let's say the rhyme again!

2 💬 **Learn the rhyme.**

 **At school**

In class

1 🔊 **Listen and point.**

Look at the board.

I've got an orange ruler.

pencil
pencil case
ruler
pen
book
schoolbag

My favourite book

Eric · Phil · Tim · Emily · Liz · Sally · Susan

I've got =
I have got

2 👥 **What school things have you got?**
Tell your partner: I've got a ...

⭐ **Make your own picture dictionary.**
Draw and write.

pen

School in England

I can see …

On the photo, I can see …

 1 💬 **Talk about the photos.**

in class

pupils in school uniform

lunchtime

a lollipop lady

 2 💿 **Listen and read.**

Hello, my name is Ella. I'm 9.
I go to Westminster School. I'm in class 3 c.
My teacher is Mrs Black.
My school uniform is red and white.
School starts at 9 o'clock in the morning
and ends at 4 o'clock in the afternoon.
I like music and sports.
What about you?

 3 **What about your school day? Do a presentation.**

Head and shoulders

Head   and shoul-ders, knees and   toes,   knees   and toes.   Head   and shoul-ders,

knees   and   toes,   knees   and   toes____   and____   eyes   and   ears   and

mouth_   and__   nose,   head   and shoul-ders, knees and   toes,   knees   and toes.

1 Sing the song and do the actions.

2 Sing the song faster and faster.

3 Sing and drop the word [head].
Sing again and drop the words [head] **and** [shoulders] ...

Hm and shoulders, knees ...

Hm and hm, knees ...

one knee – two knee**s**

Ouch!

1 **Read the comic.**

Snakes and ladders

1 Play the game. Do the actions.

Roll the dice. Do the actions.

 Correct action 🙂 : Go up the ladder.

 Wrong action ☹ : Go down the snake.

 Sally's hotspot:

Correct action 🙂 : Roll the dice again.

Wrong action ☹ : Go back to the start.

one foot –
two feet

---

3 Touch your head.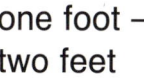

8 Bend your knees.

16 Sing: Head and shoulders …

19 Wash your hands.

24 Count your fingers.

27 Shake your feet.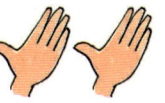

29 Stretch your arms.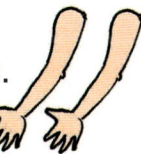

33 Point to your eyes.

43 Touch your ears.

48 Stretch your legs.

52 Brush your hair.

58 Say: Good morning!

59 Point to your nose.

62 Shake your body.

Monster, monster how do you feel?

happy

angry

scared

sad

tired

1  **Listen, point and say:** The yellow monster is …

2 **Draw your own monster and write.** My monster is …

Tim's wish list

spaceship £17

£20 helicopter ✗

helmet £90 bike £30

£100 £200 helmet £40 ✗ bike ✗

castle £80

£10 doll

£18 racing car football £8

£1 rubber £5 book

£2 ruler pencils £3 ✗

1 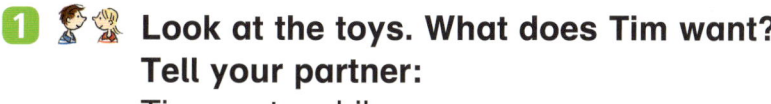 **Look at the toys. What does Tim want?**
Tell your partner:
Tim wants a bike ...

2  **Ask your partner:** How much is the ...?

3 **Make a wish list for your class and discuss.**
We want to buy ...

I want –
Tim want**s**

The fish who could wish

In the deep blue sea, in the deep of the blue,
swam a fish who could wish, and each wish would come true.

He wished for a castle.

He wished for a car.

He wished for a horse and a Spanish guitar.

One day, just for fun, that silly old fish,
wished the silliest, silliest wish he could wish.

That silly old fish wished he could be
just like all the other fish in the sea.

But wishing was something other fish could not do.
So that was his very last wish that came true.

1 🔘 **Listen and point.**

2 👦👧 **Look at the pictures.**
Tell the story to your partner.

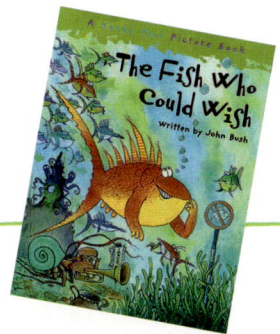

Sally in the snow

1 💿 **Listen to the story.**

2 🗨 **Look and say:** Sally put**s** on her … / Sally take**s** off her …

T-shirt

socks

trousers

pullover

boots

jacket

scarf

woolly hat

gloves

Rrring!

Hi, Sally!

Hello!

3 Do the clothes rally.

What's the weather like?

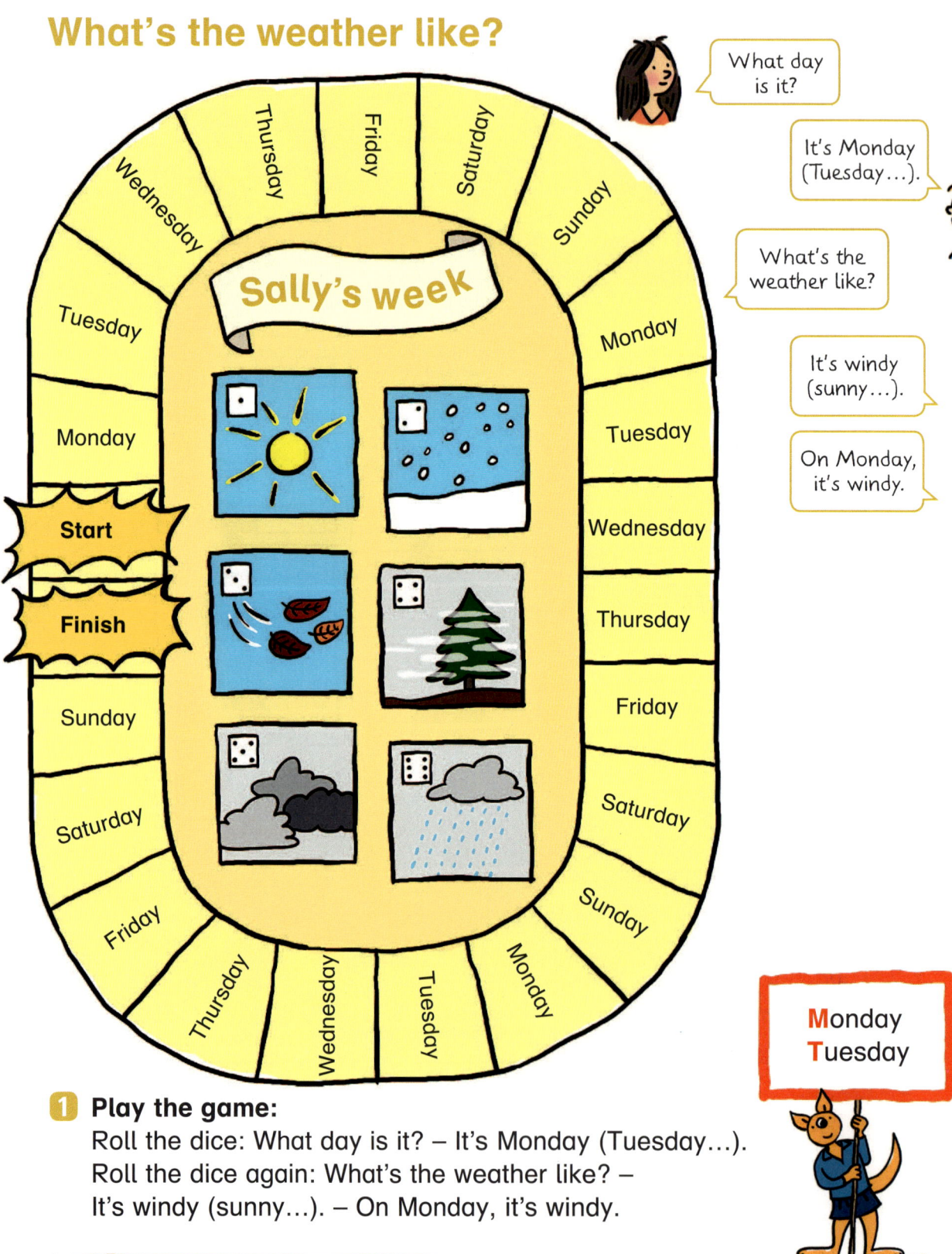

What day is it?

It's Monday (Tuesday...).

What's the weather like?

It's windy (sunny...).

On Monday, it's windy.

Monday
Tuesday

1 **Play the game:**
Roll the dice: What day is it? – It's Monday (Tuesday...).
Roll the dice again: What's the weather like? –
It's windy (sunny...). – On Monday, it's windy.

The wind and the sun

1. 💬 **Look at the picture. What can you see?**

2. 💿🧒🧒 **Listen to the story. Tell it to your partner.**

3. 👨‍👧‍👦 **Act out the story in your group.**

The weather forecast

1. 💬 **Talk about the picture.**

2. 💿💬 **What's the weather like? Listen, point and tell.**

3. 🐕 **What's the weather like in Paris, in Hamburg …?**
   Look in a newspaper or on the Internet.
   Make a weather forecast in your group
   and do a presentation.

⭐ **Make a weather chart for one week.**

Presentation tips:
• Speak loudly and clearly.
• Look at the class.
• Show pictures.

CD 1.32

Happy birthday

Birthday invitation

Dear Susan,
Please come to my birthday party.

When: Saturday, 5 March at 2 o'clock
Where: 25, Main Street
Phone: 3472

Can you come to my party?
Yours, Emily

January	February	March 5 Emily
April	May	June
July	August	September
October	November	December

HAPPY BIRTHDAY

1 💬 **Talk about Emily's birthday party.**

2 💬 **How do you celebrate your birthday? Tell your class.**

3 🐶 **Make a birthday calendar.**

4 ✏️ **Write a birthday invitation.**

January
February

Keith Haring

the artist

"Best buddies"

"Football"

"Group"

1  **Look at the pictures.**
Describe the colours and actions.

group work

presentation

"Dancing in the sun"

"Friends"

2 **Make a picture about friends:**
1. Cut out different figures.
2. Glue them on coloured paper.
3. Trace your figures with a black pen.

My family

my mum and dad

my brother Tim

my grandma and grandpa

Can you find my grandma and grandpa?

aunt Helen

Can you find my mum and Tim?

Can you find aunt Helen?

This is my family!

1 **Look and point.**

What is it?

tea, coke, orange juice, coffee, hot chocolate, milk

1 Look and guess.

At the drinks stand

What would you like to drink?

I'd like a glass of water, please.

2 Look and read.

3 Make your own drinks stand. Act out the scene.

4 Make a poster about drinks.

The magic trick

I can do magic!
I can read your
thoughts!

A.

B.

D.

C.

CORN FLAKES

1 Do the trick.

2 Can you do a magic trick?
Show your class.

1 orange juice	8 hot chocolate
2 honey	9 jam
3 tea	10 cheese
4 toast	11 egg
5 ham	12 coffee
6 water	13 milk
7 bread	14 roll
	15 cornflakes

My favourite breakfast

everyday breakfast

traditional cooked breakfast

1 💬 **Look and speak.**

2 👦👧 **Ask your partner.**

3 **What do you have for breakfast?**
For breakfast, I have …

4 **Do the breakfast rally.**

At the ice cream stand

Can I help you?

cherry

banana

pear

vanilla

chocolate

lemon

strawberry

orange

pineapple

I'd like …

1 🔊💬 **Listen and speak.**

2 👦👧 **Ask your partner:**
What's your favourite ice cream?

Let's make a smoothie

1 **Look and read.**

This is what you need.

Wash the strawberries.

Peel the bananas.

Cut the fruit.

Put them into the jug.

Add water or milk.

Mix it.

Pour the smoothie into your glass.

Enjoy!

2 **Make your own smoothie.**

Little dog lost

Little dog lost
We miss Bobby
Little dog lost
We miss Bobby very much.
Tim and Susan Brown
phone: 9856

1 **Listen. Where is Bobby?**

These pets have new homes

dog

Jack and Mr Tailor

rabbit

Hopsy and Sophie Miller

cat

Tippy and Mrs Davis

guinea pig

Molly and Kevin Fisher

tortoise

Rocky and Sammy Baker

hamster

Fred and Alice Smith

budgie

Charlie and Mrs Cooper

1 Listen, look and speak.

2 Make a missing pet report.

3 Act it out with your partner.

mouse

Speedy

The wheels on the bus

1. The wheels on the bus go round and round,
   round and round, round and round.
   The wheels on the bus go round and round,
   all around the town.

2. The wipers on the bus
   go "Swish, swish, swish" …

3. The horn on the bus goes "Beep, beep, beep" …

4. The driver on the bus says "Move on back!" …

5. The baby on the bus says "Wah, wah, wah!" …

6. The mummy on the bus says "Shh, shh, shh" …

1 **Listen, sing and act.**

 Write your own verse. Use your dictionary.

Let's go to London!

the Royal Family

guards

Buckingham Palace

Tower Bridge

the London Eye

Big Ben

1 Look at the photos.

2 Make a poster about London sights.

I want to be a queen!

Farm animals

Clumsy the dog

At night …

The next morning …

Who stole the eggs?

Clumsy, was that you?

In the evening …

Me? No, it wasn't me. Not this time!

But Clumsy, you always say that.

It wasn't me … Why don't they believe me?

The next morning …

Wake up! It wasn't Clumsy. Look!

Hold the thief!

Clumsy, good thing you are so clumsy!

Oops!

1 **Listen to the story.**

2 **Read the story.**

Alphabet rhyme

A B C D E F G,
on the farm there is a bee.

H I J K L M N,
it lands directly on a hen.

O P Q R S T U,
and asks her friendly:
"How are you?"

V W X Y Z,
"I'm fine, but please,
get off my head."

1 💿 **Listen and point.**

2 **Read the rhyme.**

3 **Do the animal rally.**

On the beach

She sells seashells on the seashore.

1. 💬 **Look and speak. How many seashells can you find?**

2. 🐾 **Create your own summer exhibition in groups. Use your dictionary. Present it to your class.**

Robin Hood's game

1 Play the game.

Robin Hood

17

Look!
The sheriff is coming.
Go to 16.

18

19

Wave to the farmer.
Go to 37.

35

Have breakfast
on the farm.
Miss a turn.

34

36

20

33

37

21

22

23

32

Drink some milk.
Go to 34.

38

Hide
behind
the tree.
Go to 19.

ok at
castle.
l the dice again.

31

39

30

40

29

7

28

41

Give money to the poor.
Go to 31.

42

FINISH

Rush hour

The ghost

I saw a ghost.
He saw me, too.
I waved at him.
But he said "Boo!".

Boo!

Tongue twister

Two witches are watching two watches.
Which witch is watching which watch?

1 Look and read.
Can you say the tongue twister?

⭐ Choose a witch and describe her to your partner.

It's Halloween

1 🖸 **Listen to the song.**

2 🖸 **Listen to the story.**

⭐ **Act out the story.**

Christmas Eve

1 **Look and find these Christmas things:**
mistletoe, Christmas tree, stockings, Christmas cards, presents

2 **Listen to the story.**

3 **How do you celebrate Christmas?**

I hear them

I hear them, I hear them, I hear them on the roof!
The rein-deer are com-ing, I hear each pranc-ing hoof!
With a jin-gle, jin-gle bell and a clop, clop, clop
and a clat-ter, clat-ter, clat-ter at the chim-ney top.
I hear them, I hear them, I hear them on the roof!

1  Listen to the song.

2 Sing the song.

3 Act out the song.

4 Make a Christmas card.

CD 2.34

Make your own Christmas stocking

You need:
thick brown paper, a pencil,
scissors, glue, a hole punch,
wool, felt tips or wax crayons
and coloured paper

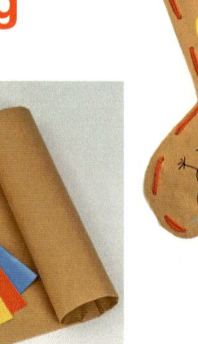

Draw a large stocking
on the thick brown paper.
Cut out two copies of the stocking.

Glue the two stockings
together around the edges.
Leave the top open.

Punch holes around the edges
of the stocking.
Weave wool in and out of the holes.

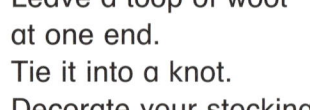

Leave a loop of wool
at one end.
Tie it into a knot.
Decorate your stocking.

1 **Look and read.**

2  **Create your own stocking.**

 Describe your stocking.

Valentine's cards

1 **Read the comic.**

2 **Read the rhymes. What's your favourite rhyme?**

In February
it's Valentine's Day.
I write Valentine's cards
to my friends.

Candy is sweet,
this is true,
but for my Valentine
I'll choose you.

I like you!
Be my Valentine!

Jingle, jangle,
silver bangle,
you look fit
from every angle.

Roses are red,
violets are blue,
sugar is sweet
and so are you!

3  **Make your own Valentine's card.**

Edgar's Easter eggs

1 💿 **Listen to the story. Act it out.**

2 💬 **Where are the Easter eggs? Look and tell.**

3 **Look and read.**

You need:
a toilet roll, white paper, pink paper,
glue, scissors, felt tips or coloured pencils,
pipe cleaners

Cover the toilet roll
with white paper.

Draw a bunny face
on it.

Cut out two ears from the
white paper and the centres
from the pink paper.

Glue on the ears.

Glue on the
pipe cleaners.

4 **Make your own Easter egg cup.**

Hello   Hallo

boy   Junge

girl   Mädchen

children   Kinder

basketball   Basketball

computer game   Computerspiel

inline skating   Inlineskaten

singing   Singen

skateboard   Skateboard

tennis   Tennis

Hello./Hi.   Hallo.

Good morning.   Guten Morgen.

How are you? – I'm fine, thanks.
Wie geht es dir? – Danke, gut.

What's your name? – My name is ...
Wie heißt du? – Ich heiße …

What do you like? –
I like … And you?
Was magst du? –
Ich mag … Und du?

I can see (a) ...   Ich sehe (ein/e) ...

Colours and numbers
Farben und Zahlen

black   schwarz

blue   blau

brown   braun

green   grün

grey   grau

orange   orange

pink   rosa, pink

purple   lila

red   rot

white   weiß

yellow   gelb

one   eins

two   zwei

three   drei

four   vier

five   fünf

six   sechs

seven   sieben

eight   acht

nine   neun

ten   zehn

What colour is it? –
It's green (blue ...).
Welche Farbe hat es? –
Es ist grün (blau …).

What's your telephone number? –
My telephone number is …
Wie lautet deine Telefonnummer? –
Meine Telefonnummer ist …

At school   In der Schule

(black)board   Tafel

book   Buch

class   Klasse

classroom   Klassenzimmer

computer   Computer

folder   Ordner

glue stick   Klebestift

lollipop lady   Schülerlotsin

pen   Füller

pencil   Bleistift

pencil case   Federmäppchen

pencil sharpener   Spitzer

pupil   Schüler

rubber   Radiergummi

ruler   Lineal

school   Schule

schoolbag   Schultasche

school things   Schulsachen

school uniform   Schuluniform

(a pair of) scissors   eine Schere

teacher   Lehrer(in)

in   in

on   auf

under   unter

I've got a …   Ich habe ein(e, en) …

I go to Westminster School.
Ich gehe in die Westminster-Schule.

I'm in class 3c.
Ich bin in der Klasse 3c.

My teacher is Mrs/Mr …
Meine Lehrerin / Mein Lehrer
heißt Frau/Herr …

Body and feelings
Körper und Gefühle

arm   Arm

body   Körper

ear   Ohr

eye   Auge

face   Gesicht

finger   Finger

foot – feet   Fuß – Füße

hair   Haar

hand   Hand

head   Kopf

knee   Knie

leg   Bein

mouth   Mund

nose   Nase

shoulder   Schulter

toe   Zeh

tooth – teeth   Zahn – Zähne

angry   zornig

fine   gut

happy   glücklich

sad   traurig

scared   verängstigt, erschrocken

tired   müde

How do you feel? – I'm happy/sad …
Wie fühlst du dich? – Ich bin
glücklich/traurig …

I'm okay.   Mir geht's ganz gut.

Toys   Spielzeug

big   groß

car   Auto

castle   Burg, Schloss

children   Kinder

computer game   Computerspiel

doll   Puppe

fish   Fisch

football   Fußball

guitar   Gitarre

helicopter   Hubschrauber

helmet   Helm

horse   Pferd

bike   Fahrrad

racing car   Rennauto

small   klein

spaceship   Raumschiff

teddy bear   Teddybär

(to) want   wollen

(to) wish (for)   sich wünschen

eleven   elf

twelve   zwölf

thirteen   dreizehn

fourteen   vierzehn

fifteen   fünfzehn

sixteen   sechzehn

seventeen   siebzehn

eighteen   achtzehn

nineteen   neunzehn

twenty   zwanzig

British   britisch

money   Geld

penny – pence (p)   Penny – Pence

pound (£)   Pfund

How much is the ...? –
The ... is ... pounds.
Wie viel kostet der (die, das) ...? –
Der (die, das) ... kostet ... Pfund.

How much is it? – It's ... pounds.   Wie
viel kostet das? – Das macht ... Pfund.

Tim/Susan wants …
Tim/Susan möchte …

Clothes   Kleidung

boots   Stiefel

cap   Kappe

coat   Mantel

dress   Kleid

gloves   Handschuhe

jacket   Jacke

(a pair of) jeans   eine Jeans

pullover   Pullover

(to) put on   anziehen

scarf   Schal

shirt   Hemd

shoes   Schuhe

(a pair of) shorts
eine kurze Hose, Shorts

skirt   Rock

socks   Socken

(to) take off   ausziehen

(a pair of) trousers   eine Hose

T-shirt   T-Shirt

(to) wear   tragen, anhaben

woolly hat   Mütze

For my holidays, I pack …
Für meine Ferien packe ich … ein.

Sally puts on her … / takes off her …
Sally zieht ihr(e, en) … an/aus.

Weather and days
Wetter und Tage

Monday   Montag

Tuesday   Dienstag

Wednesday   Mittwoch

Thursday   Donnerstag

Friday   Freitag

Saturday   Samstag

Sunday   Sonntag

day   Tag

week   Woche

cloud/y   Wolke/wolkig

cold   kalt

fog/gy   Nebel/neblig

hot   heiß

rain/y   Regen/regnerisch

snow/y   Schnee/verschneit

sun/ny   Sonne/sonnig

weather forecast   Wettervorhersage

wind/y   Wind/windig

When can we meet? – We can meet on Monday (Tuesday …).   Wann können wir uns treffen? – Wir können uns am Montag (Dienstag …) treffen.

What day is it? – It's Monday. (Tuesday ...).   Welchen Tag haben wir? – Es ist Montag (Dienstag ...).

What's the weather like today? – Today it's windy (sunny …).
Wie ist das Wetter heute? – Heute ist es windig (sonnig …).

On Monday, it's sunny.
Am Montag ist es sonnig.

Around the year
Rund ums Jahr

January   Januar
February   Februar
March   März
April   April
May   Mai
June   Juni
July   Juli
August   August
September   September
October   Oktober
November   November
December   Dezember
month   Monat

spring   Frühling
summer   Sommer
autumn   Herbst
winter   Winter
season   Jahreszeit

balloon   Ballon
birthday   Geburtstag
cake   Torte, Kuchen
calendar   Kalender
candle   Kerze
card   Karte
crown   Krone
guest   Gast
invitation   Einladung
party   Party, Feier
present   Geschenk

When's your birthday? –
My birthday is in …
Wann ist dein Geburtstag? –
Mein Geburtstag ist im …

Happy birthday!
Alles Gute zum Geburtstag!

How old are you? – I'm eight (years old).
Wie alt bist du? –
Ich bin acht (Jahre alt).

Family and friends
Familie und Freunde

aunt   Tante
boy   Junge
brother   Bruder
family   Familie
father/dad   Vater/Papa
friend   Freund(in)
girl   Mädchen
grandfather/grandpa   Großvater/Opa
grandmother/grandma
Großmutter/Oma
mother/mum   Mutter/Mama
sister   Schwester
uncle   Onkel

My best friend is ...
Mein(e) beste(r) Freund(in) ist …

He/She is … years old.
Er/Sie ist … Jahre alt.

He/She has got ...   Er/Sie hat …

Have you got brothers or sisters? –
I've got ... / I haven't got ...
Hast du Geschwister? –
Ich habe … / Ich habe keine …

This is my family. /
These are my friends.
Das ist meine Familie. /
Dies sind meine Freunde.

 Drinks   Getränke

coffee   Kaffee
coke   Cola
hot chocolate   Kakao
lemonade   Limonade
(a glass of) milk   (ein Glas) Milch
orange juice   Orangensaft
(a cup of) tea   (eine Tasse) Tee
water   Wasser

What drinks do you like? – I like …
Welche Getränke magst du? –
Ich mag …

I like … best.   Am liebsten mag ich …

What drinks don't you like? –
I don't like …
Welche Getränke magst du nicht? –
Ich mag kein(e, en) …

What would you like to drink? –
I'd like …, please.   Was würdest du
gerne trinken? – Ich hätte gerne …, bitte.

 Breakfast   Frühstück

bread   Brot
breakfast   Frühstück
butter   Butter
cheese   Käse
cornflakes   Cornflakes
(to) drink   trinken
(to) eat   essen
egg   Ei
ham   Schinken
honey   Honig
jam   Marmelade
roll   Brötchen
toast   Toast

What do you have for breakfast?
Was isst/trinkst du zum Frühstück?

For breakfast, I have …
Zum Frühstück esse/trinke ich …

Do you like …? –
Yes, I do. / No, I don't.
Magst du …? – Ja. / Nein.

Can I have the …, please? –
Here you are.   Kann ich bitte den/die/
das … haben? – Hier, bitte.

 Fruit   Obst

apple   Apfel
banana   Banane
cherry   Kirsche
fruit   Frucht, Obst
lemon   Zitrone
melon   Melone
orange   Orange, Apfelsine
pear   Birne

pineapple   Ananas
plum   Pflaume
strawberry   Erdbeere
tree   Baum

(to) add   hinzufügen
(to) cut   schneiden
ice cream   Eiskrem
ice cream stand   Eisstand
jug   Krug
(to) mix   mischen
(to) peel   schälen
(to) pour   eingießen
(to) put   hineingeben, legen, stellen
scoop   Eiskugel
smoothie   Smoothie, Fruchtshake
(to) wash   waschen

What's your favourite ice cream?
Was ist dein Lieblingseis?

Can I help you?
Kann ich dir/euch/Ihnen helfen?

I'd like … – Here you are.
Ich hätte gerne … – Hier, bitte.

That's … pounds, please. – Thank you.
Das macht bitte … Pfund. – Danke.

Goodbye.   Auf Wiedersehen.

 **Pets**   Haustiere

bird   Vogel
budgie   Wellensittich
cat   Katze
dog   Hund
fish   Fisch(e)
guinea pig   Meerschweinchen
hamster   Hamster

mouse – mice   Maus – Mäuse
pet   Haustier
rabbit   Kaninchen
tail   Schwanz
tortoise   Schildkröte
wing   Flügel

What's your favourite pet?
Was ist dein Lieblingshaustier?

My favourite pet is a …
Mein Lieblingshaustier ist ein(e) …

Its name is …   Es heißt …

Can I help you? – I've lost my pet.
Kann ich dir/euch/Ihnen helfen? – Ich
habe mein Haustier verloren.

What colour is it? – It's black
(brown …).
Welche Farbe hat es? – Es ist
schwarz (braun …).

 London   London

bus   Bus
bus driver   Busfahrer
England   England
guard   Wache, Wachposten
king   König
(to) move   bewegen, sich bewegen
palace   Palast
prince   Prinz
princess   Prinzessin
queen   Königin
Royal Family   Königsfamilie
sight   Sehenswürdigkeit

I want to be a …   Ich will ein(e) … sein.

I want to see …   Ich will … sehen.

Farm animals
Bauernhoftiere

animal   Tier

barn   Stall

bee   Biene

clumsy   ungeschickt

cow   Kuh

duck   Ente

farm   Bauernhof

farmer   Bauer

goose – geese   Gans – Gänse

hen   Huhn, Henne

horse   Pferd

pig   Schwein

sheep   Schaf, Schafe

What's your favourite animal? –
It's a …
Was ist dein Lieblingstier? –
Es ist ein(e) …

Summer   Sommer

airbed   Luftmatratze

beach   Strand

beach ball   Wasserball

(to) build   bauen

holidays   Ferien

ice cream   Eiskrem

(to) play   spielen

sand   Sand

sandcastle   Sandburg

sea   Meer

seashell   Muschel

(to) snorkel   schnorcheln

suncream   Sonnenkrem

sunglasses   Sonnenbrille

(to) swim   schwimmen

towel   Handtuch

How many … can you see/find? –
I can see/find …
Wie viele … kannst du sehen/finden? –
Ich kann … sehen/finden.

Robin Hood   Robin Hood

arrow   Pfeil

bow   Bogen

castle   Burg, Schloss

(to) catch   fangen

(to) dress up   sich verkleiden

forest   Wald

hat   Hut

(to) play a trick
einen Streich spielen

poor   arm

rich   reich

(to) ride (a horse)
(ein Pferd) reiten

sheriff   Sheriff

(to) shoot   schießen

Help!   Hilfe!

Hands up!   Hände hoch!

Happy Halloween
Fröhliches Halloween

bat   Fledermaus

broom   Besen

costume   Kostüm, Verkleidung

dark   dunkel

door   Tür

ghost   Geist, Gespenst

Halloween   Halloween

hat   Hut

house   Haus

(to) knock   klopfen

monster   Ungeheuer, Monster

moon   Mond

night   Nacht

pumpkin   Kürbis

(to) shake   schütteln

skeleton   Gerippe, Skelett

star   Stern

sweets   Süßigkeiten

witch   Hexe

Happy Halloween!
Fröhliches Halloween!

It's eight (nine …) o'clock.
Es ist acht (neun …) Uhr.

Trick or treat!   Süßes oder Saures!

 ## Merry Christmas
Frohe Weihnachten

bell   Glocke

carrot   Karotte

chimney   Schornstein

Christmas card   Weihnachtskarte

Christmas Eve   Heiligabend,
Weihnachtsabend

Christmas tree   Weihnachtsbaum

Father Christmas   Weihnachtsmann

fireplace   (offener) Kamin

(to) get presents   Geschenke
bekommen

hungry   hungrig

mistletoe   Mistel(zweig)

reindeer   Rentier(e)

sleigh   Schlitten

snowman   Schneemann

stocking   Strumpf

Merry Christmas!   Frohe Weihnachten!

 ## Valentine's Day
Valentinstag

Valentine's Day   Valentinstag

(to) write Valentine's cards
Valentinskarten schreiben

It's Valentine's Day.
Es ist Valentinstag.

I like you.   Ich mag dich.

 ## Happy Easter   Frohe Ostern

basket   Korb

bush   Busch

(to) colour   färben, anmalen

Easter bunny   Osterhase

Easter egg   Osterei

Easter egg cup   Ostereierbecher

fence   Zaun

fun   Spaß

happy   glücklich

(to) hide   verstecken

sad   traurig

(to) share   teilen

behind   hinter

in   in

in front of   vor

on   auf

under   unter

Happy Easter!   Frohe Ostern!

Is the yellow (red …) egg in/on/under
the …?
Ist das gelbe (rote …) Ei in/auf/unter
dem/der …?